what counts

This work is licensed under a Creative Commons
Attribution-NoDerivs 3.0 Unported License

2012 Fred Andrle
Some rights reserved

Book design by Jerry Kelly

Cover photograph by Fred Andrle:
Lunar Halo, December 8, 2011, Columbus, Ohio

Woodcut *Earth, Sea and Sky* by Marlene Hyman

Printed by UniPrint
The Ohio State University

First printing July 2012
Printed in USA

ISBN 978-1-880977-33-0

This publication was made possible by the generous support of
The Ohio State University Humanities Institute.

what counts

poems
fred andrle

xoxox
PRESS

What Counts

Seasons

An Invitation 9
Waiting for the Moon 10
Football Tempest 11
Rapscallion Summer 13
Autumn Break 15
All Hallowed 16
Early Spring, Iraq Notwithstanding 17
Thaw 18
Autumn Hymn 22
Tonight, Rain 23
Moon Lover 24
Woof! 27
Autumn Too Soon 28
Winter Holiday 29
Farmer's Market 31
So Long, Winter-pal 32

Journeys

The Journey 35
The New Road 36
Kid 38
Flood 40
Pictures 42
On the Gerontological Road 44
Voyagers 45

What Counts

What Counts 47
If I Knew 48
So What? Here's What! 49
Trouble 51
Why? 53
Daemon 54
Healer 56
Conscientious Defector 58
To a Sour Lover 59
Tick-tock 60
Buyer's Market 62
You Always Have an Answer 64
If 65
So What's Up? 66

To My Walking Pneumonia 68
Biding Time 69
O!H!!!O! 70
Life's a... 71
Joy to the World 73
Shame on You? 75
Eclipsed 76
About Face 77
Measure Up! 78
Born-again 79
Let's Get Mad 80
Your Day 82
Winter Instant 83
Stop. Please. 85
Counseling Our Youth 87
That's Life/Death 88
Pause 90

Departures

God's Loss 92
Wings 93
Death Uncomprehended 95
When My Father Died 97
When I Go 98
Fisherman Eternal 99
The Death Interviews 101
At Any Moment 103
A Prayer for the Last Day 105
My Heavens! 106

Especially for Poets

You're a Poet—Too Bad for You! 109
Poet's Lament 110
Successful Writers All Leave the Midwest 111
To the Writer Turning 70 112
I'm Serious Serious 114
Packing Up the Bookstore 115
Publish, Perish 116

Best of Fred

Spring Moon 119
Heaven's Little Western New York Helper 120
Winter Boys 121
To My Brother on His Magic Farm 123
To My Father, Empowered By a Stroke 124
The Book 126

For Marlene

Seasons

An Invitation

There's a rain arriving from the mysterious west
it will patter against the dog-faced mimosa leaves
stream down along the asphalt shingles
splash into your pink and upturned mouth.

It's the very same as the childhood rains
that happily soaked you as you ran barefoot
down the hissing sidewalks
to the muddy schoolyard

where seasoned earth caressed your feet
warm drops trickling down your original face
rivulets along the skin of you naked to the waist
and the morning passed without explanation.

Cardinals chirruped in the dripping maples
young squirrels cavorted in the loamy yards
crows called out their predictions from building tops
and the rain kept falling and you did not retreat.

That all-day shower is here again
inviting you back into the quieting alleys
nourishing the bold hollyhocks that delight you
awaiting only your upside smile, your carefree affirmation.

Waiting for the Moon

I'll be staying up very late for the moon
you know the one I mean, the moon that's gleaming
the moon that's proud to bustle overhead
every bit as pleased as a moon can be.

You know that moon, you'd know him any night
molding his body from fat to sliver
soaring along in the celestial stillness
shaking up the oceans and the tides.

You understand this moon is here to stay
you know this brother's chortling in his flight
confident he'll be there many moons from now
long past the sun that finally sizzles out.

Say hello to the moon for me
he's got it made, that impudent eternal guy
far beyond our inch-long lives
he'll cheer our children's many children.

Mister Moon of song and rhyme
of jumping cows and dreamy window gazing
he's worth the wait, he'll hurl us out
far past despair and wistful yearning.

Let's toast his headlong, measured flight
he'll meet us here most any night
to loft us on a salty trip
where mortal minds and bodies do not fail.

So pack a bag, bring your umbrella
we'll meet that cheery, wayward fella
flick away the evening's darkness
sail away upon his easeful light.

Football Tempest

September storm approaching from the west
Buckeye Saturday, we're all indoors
the TVs watch the street, we're turned away
the storm breaks loud, a touchdown yell prevails.

Maybe gales could charm us if we knew
that rain is splashing asphalt like king's crowns
that if we'd open sealed front doors a crack,
we'd sniff some tangy ozone like a kid.

A word about those kids: they're indoors, too,
playing upstairs touchdown iTouch contests
learning how to fight, to shoot and kill
while parents (victims?) scan the bruising game.

Our dogs would cheer the rolling wind and rain
if anybody'd leash them for a stroll
they're lying flat on beery kitchen floors
they sigh and sleep, all canine hope extinguished.

The storm is grumbling harsh now, throwing bolts
of lightning that disrupt the TV picture
we note the tempest, rave against the rain,
hope the power won't go out, fourth quarter.

Outside a grievous wind decides to twist,
down the block a tree's yanked up from life
it splits across the roadway, blocking lanes
but nobody approaches, tie ball game.

We're daft in overtime, the storm's exhausted
it drifts away, dispersing to the east
the drains inhale the muddy water pooled
the sun makes haste to dry and warm our cars.

12 Our victory achieved, we're snack food sotted
we've tamed the firmament, controlled for ease
we'll march out to a day forged just for us
the storm, our past, has lost the power to terrify or please.

Rapscallion Summer

We piked dog crap on sticks
chased each other, whooping,
never minded where we wallowed,
our britches rank and grimy.

We pooped in window wells
wiped with Elephant Ears
loped away, chortling
collapsed under concealing willows.

We ran from slow Santos guarding school construction
spat down from the choir loft on Carmelite novena-goers
pushed Kevin Kell in through the milk box
grabbed up Bowman baseball cards and ran like hell.

Down at Klaiber's delicatessen purloining Grapesicles,
yelling through St. Mary's sanctuary
stranding proud American flags
knotting the ropes that hauled them down.

Seeking bold opportunity
on the night streets where we plied our mischief trade,
we pulled strings taut over summer evening sidewalks
flipped glowing pipes out of startled mouths.

We were the rollicking boys, thefting dad's spyglass
watching Arlene Gummins strip down to her brassiere
at her bedroom window, then she pulled down the shades
and we didn't know what masturbation was.

14 We moaned in the evening bushes, panicking Barbara Wood
told Sally Morgan only Catholics go to heaven
jammed a box of honeybees in Muck Fassett's mailbox
leaped out grinning onto wailing diesel rails.

Hissing out bicycle air in night garages
Scotch-taping thumbtacks to sisters' chairs
billowing up sun-fires with magnifying glasses
dirt-warring, one side of Blantyre Road against the other.

We were rough boys till the stars popped out
taming us with the awesome Dipper
but we plotted in our night beds, whispering with the radio
clutched to our ears till we passed into innocent sleep.

Autumn Break

A sudden halt in chilly winter's march
a cockeyed sun loops down the western sky
every bull and beagle energized
for this last hour before the icy plunge.

Young kids in their shirtsleeves toss footballs
as elders, half-suspicious of unexpected warmth,
rock on, faces mild, shoulders high,
their young replacements laughing in the day.

The last holdout maples brandish leaves
Motorcycle Tom out for an exit ride
everybody open and lazy and delighted
backyard mud burps up a dank perfume.

We all know what's churning, swiftly arriving
oaks will be shutting down their limbs
but we've got one day to saunter down the path
till sodden blasts dismember our enjoyment.

There's a red-sweatered girl in the alley
she's prancing along like she's headed toward spring
Buddy the next door wolf-dog croons with passing sirens
big river carp are leaping, slapping back against the water.

A sound like wind is passing through the neighborhood
a courier of chill to come
but we turn our backs on beckoning shadows
we leap around the lawn like sunny May.

It's a temporary healing we've needed
a last defiant lark before a season of travail
through deep night we'll remember and give thanks
for the favor of this live and lusty day.

All Hallowed

Halloween's a-coming, chortling down the block
children waltzing in the streets
and grand ghosts in the hedges
shimmering and wailing in the leaves.

It's Halloween when souls are limpid
spells are cast by the kitchen door
little Mary charming like an angel
Stephen stamping peg-legged down the corridor.

It's All Hallows Eve, the dead are shining
brighter than the sun at summer's noon
begging from us favors, shibboleths and candy
as they whistle down the block, reborn.

Halloween, they're hanging in the trees
whispering to living spirits of mortals
reminding us that skeletons press outward
that our gravesite earth is wearing terribly thin.

Halloween, one evening of easy permission
for the living to hang out with the dead
blunting the message of rotting corpses
letting us know it's all OK beyond.

We'll take this message back to our mundane daily chore
our appointment with the saints already made
treasuring this evening of ghostly interweaving
as we munch the apple, lick the candy bar.

We'll fly this Halloween on brooms of spooky witches
leave our inky mark upon the pillar and the floor
watch this holy night with guardian jack-o'-lanterns
till dawn sweeps in and binds us fast once more.

Early Spring, Iraq Notwithstanding

Buddy the wolf-dog paces in the yard
rain spits down from darkling skies
there's a chill and a rapid sun departure,
a parenthesis in spring's swollen entry.

They say a storm approaches from the west
now there's only mist and a desultory wind
a paper bag is tumbling down the drugstore alley
an unmotivated romp, a half-hearted glide.

Cycles are cooling in oily garages
stymied by slick and slithery pavement
they're drooping in the dust and dampness
longing to take you on a magic carpet ride.

Cats are crouching under splintery porches
stiff on their islands of clammy mud
dogs turn away from sodden gray lawns
back to the heart and its laboring fire.

Children are lost somewhere in the attic
pawing through boxes, shivering at the rain
pattering down on a protesting roof
as the brief afternoon wastes away.

Wreckage of a promise of a season of delight
we're trapped inside with movie and bestseller
combing the refrigerator, spellbound
by beefsticks and single-slice cheese.

Maybe that storm will bring a cleansing vision
of a spring long ago when the world sang at peace
when dogs gamboled free and the long grass sparkled
in a sun that spoke of our innocent lives.

Thaw

First warm January day, there's an icicle breeze
and the pond's no longer safe, so we'll go jump on it
you can look down and see things in the ice
a twig, a berry, the eye of a fish
we'll stamp on them, we'll break them out
ice creaking under our feet, air warm, jackets open.

The river is trying to move again
it's pushing against the jammed up floe
that groans and cracks in a wind like spring.
Ducks are stranded on the shores
they're walking on the earth this snowy morning
they know the river will win the struggle
they're ready for ice to soar into woods
and when it does we'll rescue flung fish
gasping on the land
we'll push them through the water
till their airy gills power them free.

Somehow the floe always breaks in the night
somehow you're never there to see it
but you hear it from your bed, frosty windows open,
hear the sudden crush and roar
dream of tiptoeing past your sleeping parents
dream of entering the forbidden woods,
walking among the cold stone of the new-free ice.

Even the squirrels are awake this morning
they're sending messages with broomy tails
comments about the passing of the cold, about
seeds still frozen to the ground and hard to bite.
Down the block the first indoor cat is out-of-doors
he's footing it silently over the crusty snow

eyes out for the flash of feather, claws ready for the
squeaking rodent who only wants her way in peace.

Ice is dripping from the roofs,
earth is softening in the yards
the young fathers on the block
are ruefully surveying
spring tasks to come
memories of green lawns sprouting,
sweat of hot mud under the feet.

Big river rats are sunning
on the logs at the foot of the island
they're sharing ground with the turtles
who have not been seen since summer.
The owl is sleeping in the woods,
hawk is sailing over the water,
and we're banging down the alleys,
smacking trash cans with sticks,
searching for discarded treasures
in frozen back yards, wishing we could throw
an iceball at Mr. Conliff's picture window,
but the snow's no good for packing anymore.

We foray up along the high railroad tracks
where the steam trains melt the snow
the autumn fort's still there, the door's
wide open, we push inside giggling,
someone's got half a sandwich and we eat it.
The sounds of the neighborhood are far away
the two o'clock freight from Chicago
shakes the earth, covers the sky, drowns out
our reedy voices, leaves us awestruck in its wake.

Mothers and fathers have disappeared
their only province the house and yard
they'll never find us here, we can
say what we want to say, share
every long afternoon adventure,
walk forever to the far railroad ponds,
sit on the small ledge of the trestle bridge
right under the train, while the wheels
roll safely over us.

Away with remonstrating voices
stories of legs cut off by the engines
cautions about cursing and smoking,
how to behave with girls.
We're rough boys now
and we're gathered in our pack
by the melting train yards
and will most certainly be free.

This is spring in the middle of winter
this is every young boy's hope
time to take advantage of the light
to throw down coats, to tumble down the hills,
to plan and execute twilight conspiracies.
And when the last sun gleams below icebound rushes,
the first sweet voices of mothers in the neighborhoods,
we know we're hungry and it's time to go.

At night in our beds we call to one another
through the darkened houses, our voices
carry down the streets, they open doors
and enter bedrooms. The last thing we say
final words before welcoming sleep:

See you tomorrow, meet you in the morning
in the yards, by the tracks, by the beautiful river
see you there, wear your tall boots and your mittens
bring food for our travels, leave the dog at home
this time. We'll move on out, we'll never come back
while the winter sun sparkles and the great trains
carry us to our January afternoon destiny.

Autumn Hymn

Autumn like a cathedral
of trees and sunlight in trees
dogs far barking,
the edge of cooling silence.

Autumn lovely in dying
the deep sky bearing up the hawk
crisp fallen leaves mark footsteps,
the ghost of summer moaning in the hedge.

Autumn of golden slanting light
season of whispering cattails
a dry wind from the Hebrides
carries us away into slumber.

Autumn beyond all containment
wild in the night of the half-moon
visiting our beds, lighting up dreams,
dark witches blessing all endeavor.

Autumn crooning us to sleep
carrying us into darkness and silence,
as though it is our final season
he fingers our ivory bones.

Autumn forever, if we could command it,
soaring out over a gray sea
whispering a sweet departure
dragging behind him pale winter's grasp.

Tonight, Rain

Shower and dark
lulling everyone quiet
muffling the broad lanes
asserting the earth again

melting technology
hissing out the lights
everyone pauses
in living and dying

for the rain
quenching our chattering brains
pressing us sit
bidding us sail away.

Who can forget
the favor of the rain
taking us by the hand
into the fields of the past.

Here beneath the falling water
under a sky deep as space
we rest in quietude,
no remembrance of the riotous sun.

Moon Lover

He lay stretched full against the sand
his limbs like wings against it
he had come to mark the hour
prepare a ceremony for the moon
now it was his need to wait
until the warm sun vanished.

He lay, the sun passed overhead
he lay, and felt the sun move past
one eye opened and he saw
the orange ball hanging low
above the gray and rolling ocean.
Then he felt the cool, dark wind
he heard the night birds winging
felt the press of gentle light
against his tender eyelid.

He opened wide and saw the moon
floating lazily above him
the sea was calm, the night was fair
the birds had gone, the beach was still
he stood and stroked his downy hair
he made the preparations.

Three sticks had he, he swung them wide
in lunar circles for the moon
he leaped into the air and fell
he leaped again, emboldened by the light.

The bright moon watched him,
silent figure, dancing far below
she smiled her dearest smile for him

she glowed as brightly as she dared
up he looked, and up again
he saw the shining of the moon
it hurt his eyes to see.

He held his arms aloft to her
he breathed her magic vapors in
they filled his chest
they charged his blood
up he rose into the air
the sands below him smaller still
and far below the lingering sea
farther still the curve of earth.

The moon shone down, she welcomed him
she drew him close, she drew him in
he felt his arms and legs catch fire
illumined by the flaming moon
he cried aloud and threw the sticks
straight into the soaring brightness.

The moon beamed quiet, clear and steady
felt him enter her light body
pleasured softly in his coming
slowly turned above the earth.
He felt the land move far below him
felt his body burning, fiery
made a choice for light and glory
dove into her flaming depth
and swam her burning seas.

Oh the pain, and oh, the beauty
washed with light and clung with fire
silent night below him unaware.

He sang an ancient song discovered
voices of the moon remembered
stories of her misty powers
tales of bravery and boldness
days when all the earth beheld the moon.

He lay within her lighted beauty
felt her smiling, certain presence
never did he wish to leave her
always would he serve her pleasure
ever would he swim her milky seas.

The white moon and her burning lover
dream together high above the peaceful earth
not the sun, nor stars who watch them longing
can take him from her, nor will she depart
beautiful moon and ghostly human lover
we watch you in your course throughout the night
sharing in your rapture and your loving
we breathe your fire, we tremble in your holy light.

Woof!

Raining all the day without a respite
the electric fire burns our sullen hides
the goofy dogs that traipse around our parlor
beg us undertake a walk outside.

They're ready to get chilly, muddy, skin-soaked,
won't hesitate before the threshold leap
they drag down leashes with their eager canines
they dance around until we jump their joy.

We're on the porch, the rain is lightly falling
it's cool today, this January thaw
but dogs know well the world of scents and whispers
they drag us forward to our outdoor lives.

No need to think the mutt does not experience
us fearful that the wet world is alive
we trip the awkward boulevard behind them
reluctant in our inner headstrong minds.

These spaniels, setters, dachshunds, labs and beagles
know the presence of existence well-surmised
they happily explore, they swift discover
the universe's wild and welcome ride.

They see more clear than we the constant presence
of a being we look for fitfully in dark
they do not have that fateful complication
of brain and bone and body misapplied.

So let's all learn the lesson best we're able
from beasts who lead us forward to our joy
we'll dance around the moment and discover
the path we thought had vanished from our lives.

Autumn Too Soon

Mars rules high the waning summer heavens
first harvest moon peers over the trees
night air is snappy, the color is orange
first autumn tinge, the light fails early.

Goodbye to the summer of the fortunate few
long-spent ancestors watch, melancholy
as tottering leaves lose their footing and fall
in the smoky smell of campfire nights.

Spirits down by the river are grieving
the fallen summer, the lost happy day
the earth is turning her back on the sun
the stars lean closer, clouds melt away.

Autumn's the season to bury the promises
summer, profligate, spoke, then abandoned
to cache them deep in the shivering earth
till a distant spring uncovers their graves.

Who would dare tell of the pale eye of winter
the shattered church-bell, the snowbound train
icy white vesicles, wan silver sun
foretelling an end to our mortal parade.

We bow to the moon and the imp of the harvest
tear down the fields, cart them away
abide with the night and our flickering ember
sigh on our knees for life's light to stay.

Winter Holiday

First sun strikes our winter windows
old Jack Frost is burned away
maybe there's a note of spring
in wind that sighs against the house.

Deep down the halt and frozen river
something moving, slowly thrashing,
sluggish winter carp perhaps,
ginning up December thaw.

Somewhere there's a warming plain,
beasts abroad in wilding breezes:
where Earth assumes a kindly slant
her lucky denizens dance quite naked.

We make to frolic in the chill,
feint toward a freezing river walk,
mostly chuff around indoors
pajama'd till midday.

Lots of exercise on stairways
TV mounts her weekend throne
we're sluggish in our wastrel tracks
till sleeping dark falls quickly.

There's winter books perchance to read
we're all beginning *War and Peace*
a new translation, we're so thrilled,
and we've got lots of time.

In every room, arousing heaters,
pouring out the cheer we crave,
orchestrate our season's quarrels
stoked by warmth now here, now absent.

Outside on the sledding hill
two plucky kids are skittering
on plastic sleds their fathers bought,
remembrance of their own dead past.

Mostly, children thrive indoors
entranced with playtime small, electric
held in withered childhood hands
till first alarming hint of spring.

We're ready to trudge off to work
Monday when we dig out cars
the office hosts fluorescent gloom
our bitten lives take on the glow.

Spring and summer wait in line,
in sun and earth determined queue
our bodies wane, absent delight,
winter gnaws us down to bone.

Farmer's Market

It's the last autumn neighborly outing
we won't see these amiable creatives for a while
the health stand that promises an apnea cure, guaranteed,
farm women, ruddy legs in shorts at forty degrees.

There's gluten-free, broccolini, vegan orientation,
curvy pumpkins, earth recycled, wild kombucha teas,
here come wrapped-up people in their eighties - amazing!
walking as though death weren't stepping on their heels.

There's Ernest who loves a low-power radio station nobody hears
who plays a spooky Halloween keyboard mounted on his bicycle,
Bob the home baker has perfected seven-grain bread ideal
he'll take orders, many thank yous, through the winter.

Leslie's walking her splay-legged, in-between dachshund
whose little curved back promises not to be trouble-free
there's hot spiked cider and vegetables peaked,
and the Global Village is brewing up Free Trade coffees.

It's much too flurried for cats to approach, Katia's used books
molder in the sun, the stout farm couples hawking custom beef
look like heart attacks and strokes ambulatory
and there's a willowy guy giving away free hot drinks for Jesus.

These Midwest sidewalk denizens will vanish into winter
their sprouts and leaves dormant till late spring
too bad there's not an empty hibernal market
where nothing's for sale but you greet each other's morning.

Till then this final bustling eases us into chill
we hold the memory of our friends and neighbors dear
we have faith those eighty-somethings will once again appear
when the earth to which they will return releases her new harvest bounty.

So Long, Winter-pal

You've hung around too long, brother
my skin is weary of your dry appraisal
you cloud the light, you stunt the trees
no relief from your raw breath.

Don't tell me you have tasks to be accomplished
you've cracked the streets, you've blistered walks
no reason to remain but your perverseness
if I knew a winter-begone spell I'd use it.

Can I remind you there are four seasons
each allotted a quarter of the year?
But you've been with us full five months
I could characterize this as loitering.

If I could arrest you, I'd turn out the cops
if I could boot you away I would
you tell me you assist my introspection
but I've parsed spirit sufficient for the year.

I want to frolic in something called sun
I'm sure you remember that distant star
it's a power you block so easily
I can feel you smirking around me.

I could flatter you, you've been of service
I loved your lazy white flakes falling
your crisp chill awakening me from torpor,
dark night comfort by the scented fire.

But now I need a season's greening welcome
my body craves a boulevard of budding oaks
blackbirds calling in the marsh again
light that leads me through the spread-wide-open evening.

You know that spring will overcome you
(though unlike Californians I support your presence)
so now I'll help you pack and hit the road.
Ready? Anything you've forgotten?

Journeys

The Journey

You have a compass at hand
there is a ship made ready in the harbor
the sun is rising over the far islands
you can be gone with the gathering light.

No need to wait for a signal
nor a formal announcement of departure
climb on board, your bags
are packed and waiting.

There is a stateroom assigned
the captain knows your name
there are provisions for the journey
you will be nourished and rested.

But you must learn the sails
become the crew
certain there will be storms,
the wild seas rising.

You can hunker down in your tossing room
or bind yourself to the masthead
you have the power to prevail
until the tempest's departure.

Carry on, there are treasures awaiting
and no one can tell you the nature of your gold
you will thrill at the shoreless ocean
you will journey far from mundane toil.

This is your final lifelong voyage
the one preparing you for immensity
pray each calm dawn for guidance
open your heart for a course deep and true.

The New Road

Ready for a road trip
ready for a grind:
sweet Nebraska towns
hazy under a cornfield sun

the smack downtown Sioux Falls,
fire-breathing Wall Drug T-Rex
stone Dakota Badlands
outrageous Mount Rushmore

presidents assembled,
Crazy Horse mocking
and silent Alamo, Nevada
traumatized by '50s bombs,
deep New Mexico, the ghost ranch.

Ready for a road trip into spirit
leaving careworn fantasies behind
renewing on the rocks of the Holy Cross,
in the quiet church, a mysterious organ chant.

Time for a journey that circles within
leaning toward a positive compass needle
the one that swings to all directions
the one that winds up at the center.

Off to the green forests of Maine
the loud and misty ocean shore,
night loon calling on the lake,
mild deer skirting the meadow.

And far off Oregon of the kindly people
that same ocean, rough against the sand
America, you're waiting
can I bring you my very best self?

You'll know me when you hear me coming
I'm the one wounded and despairing
I hold out my arms to you
you can lift my darkness with a touch.

Kid

The guy behind me on Southwest Airlines Flight 207
was snickering like a goat, going off every minute
a rictus, a reflex, I thought, and he must be odd, misshapen
to whinny repeatedly, dumbly, through the four-hour flight

from Columbus, Ohio to Las Vegas, chortling, multiplying
his giggles as the plane lurched and bounded down the runway
then heaved us all out into a cardboard and paste airport
jammed with burbling slot machines, deserted

by dusty travelers who had bigger stakes in mind
and I was on my way to relieve myself in a multi-colored
men's room, I could hear him marching and whickering
behind me as I hastily jammed into the deep and slippery stall.

I sat in there a while, pushing out waste, forgetting the mammal
who had pestered me for seventeen hundred miles
but when I broke out into the stale air of the C-gate section
there he was, lined up along the wall with his buddies.

I saw he was a twenty-something, portly, and right in front of me
I could watch that titter form and bleat out into the air
and I saw that he was – light-hearted - and his companions were
light-hearted and easy, smiling and joking, loose in the afternoon.

There they were amidst war, economy, earthquake, chaos
relaxed and, no fooling, happy, and his goat-laugh maybe
habit, but habit grounded in a carefree ocean of being
and I thought, let me be like this goat-man, leisurely

in a town nobody could really love, near a runway cut off from sun **39**
he was somehow hilarious in that moment, worry flown away
and I would have asked him how to snigger like a billy
if I hadn't thought it would call his attention to matters serious

make him sadly conscious of his randy and hang-loose self
so I sauntered away carrying with me nothing but a principle
over my shoulder I waved to my barnyard companion
whose rickety laugh tumbled me out grinning into a gambler's bright day.

Flood

In Johnstown, Pennsylvania, a polished bronze man
lounges near the Tribune office, thermos in hand
he is perusing a sculpted newspaper that bears
the strong-cut words: Freedom of Information.

The inclined plane chimes up and down the hill
every fifteen minutes, sometimes she's empty
cars: six dollars, you: two-fifty,
over 65, you're free, non-peak hours only.

In the inclined plane store, plastic souvenirs
an elderly woman (worked there 14 years)
has the sweetest smile, the gentlest hand
as she takes your small money and works the day.

Down in the Johnstown Chamber of Commerce
her sister in sweetness hands you a brochure
says you can visit the Flood Museum
to learn the lives of 2,000 dead.

When the big dam broke, water and flame,
in the shelter-house they thought the world was ending
for many it did, in that darkening hour
as the waters rose swift, the fires bloomed.

Don't you know Johnstown's seen better days
when the steel mills burned all night and day
the polyglot brothers earned big money
and the bars were rolling twenty-four hours.

Now she's bedraggled, this city of floods
her multiple sanctuaries closed, for sale
so Pole and Slovak, German and Irish
worship, gray heads, congregations consolidated.

The AMVETS portal needs a new coat of paint,
above the Szechuan diner, the rooms swelter dreary
and tell me about that Central City Park,
says the Commerce lady: you're lookin' at it.

Far above the city, up the hill in Westmont,
grand stone houses cool in summer heat
John, retired realtor, says there's no poverty at all
and the clipped lawns are the most beautiful in the world.

Sometimes up in Stackhouse Park
a bold city fellow picnics with his family
they yell like they don't know the park is upper-crust sacred
and they don't stay long, 'cause they're not comfortable.

The steel mills shipped to China long ago
but the library's open, there a corpulent fellow
is happy to sell you for less than a dollar
a portrait of the artist as an itinerant man.

On downtown Lincoln Street, a pink T-shirted woman:
"Sarcasm: Just One More Service I Provide"
everywhere, signs read "Watch Out for Motorcycles"
and there's Thunder in the Valley a summer weekend.

When you ride that rising/falling plane
the city primps lovely in dusky early evening
the sweet-hearted lady closes up tenderly
no word to be heard as the great moon rises.

Johnstown, you don't need any gentry uprising
to open shuttered shops for New Age boutiques
Coney Island Hots will do just fine:
Jimmy always asks, "Did you like our coleslaw?"

A little money would help and a little time
but your bright lights burn in windows when they're able
your inclined plane watches over you twenty-four hours
the rising moon comforts as best she can.

Pictures

Out along Oregon's roaring roads
where the craggy asphalt hammers your virgin tires
I saw a sign: Saturday — the True Lord's Day —
Changed by the Anti-Christ.

I looked around, Obama wasn't there
only the soft Cascade Mountains
a rolling trucker chewing foot-long jerky
he bought at the Union 76 Truck Stop

where the farmland woman at the counter
was selling Purell antiseptic hand cleaner
to a turbaned Sikh driver everybody
hadn't quite gotten used to.

He looked at me with pleading, friendless eyes
I saluted, touched my cap, he thumbed his jaunty headgear
uncertain he was, like the elderly warrior
lounging with his mutt at the Portland Area rest stop

fingering a cardboard sign: homeless & living in my van
change for food/dog food would help, God bless.
His dog was named Sweet Pea, a friendly licker,
I gave two bucks, though his van was mighty, unaffordable.

I had come from my niece's alpaca homestead
where her husband scorns her, holds her like a prisoner
the radio says NPR just fired Juan Williams
and I sigh for all the world's confusion

which is mostly, however, under my own headgear
and not in the underbrush of mountains
'cause in each journeying noggin plays a conflict picture show
about mountains, God, love, prostate cancer, sunlight.

Supposing we could let those pictures roll down U.S. #5,
leaving only the approaching: flaring autumn maples,
Nissan Cubes, sheep grazing in highway pastures,
telephone poles, rusting bridges, Rock City Pizza.

Supposing you and I could just be traveling
each person, each object, arriving original, singular,
our destination known but profoundly unknown
the whole American land stretching out before us, unadorned.

On the Gerontological Road

They tell me our fading journey is one of spirit
that we don't need the metaphorical road anymore
but I loved that highway and its possibilities
now it's rocking chair dreams, back porch fantasies.

Here I sit, droopy-eyed, dry skin withered
aging ain't for sissies, said the silver screen star.
But I saw two young guys washing down a pickup:
it had a cap, I knew they were on their way.

I wanted that adventure, but also I didn't
would I really navigate coast to stifling coast?
Whatever happened to the road of my dreams?
Is it gone with suppurating organs?

I know why they panted for the fountain of youth,
because, Friedan, my fountain of age is dry.
Though I once knew a sixty year old woman
who quit her job and bought a Chevy van.

She fixed it up for sleeping, took off into the West
said she'd begun her youth-first journey;
for a while she regaled us, we all got e-mails
then she cut us off and vanished into space.

I like to think she strode the Dakota badlands,
on a rock-hot summer day communed with scorpions
found they understood the secrets of the universe
lay flat out on a boulder and melted away.

Now I dream of that perfect capped pickup,
crimson energy soaking my greening bones
I'll drive on out to that East-West highway crossroads
Turn left? Turn right? I'll embrace my endgame way.

Voyagers

Hey, up into the high new world
out along Marley's ghost perimeter
a treasure island rich in view,
beyond the wild and lively sea.

Hey, out past our sad, dear world
into the bay of the mighty arms
led by the frolicking dog-seal bark,
nowhere clear the horizon.

Far into the mind's ancient grasp
plummeting down the hollow of winds,
along the sunset wake of evening
that's where our quest will take us.

We have a final act to perform
we're plying wisdom's journey
leaving the tracks of argument behind,
past the spirits who comfort and torment us.

Beyond even thought's powerful sway
into the streams of childhood sorrow
weaving a patient song of wholeness,
forward with prayers and dreams.

Now we sail to the far Hebrides
long past the northern villagers' complaint
evenings of ice, days of darkness
till the sun breaks over the anchor of clouds

and we rise up into the stalwart light
where we reach our promised journey's end,
releasing our final lifelong care
like the snake of the world, we shed our skins.

What Counts

What Counts

I'll count the times I laughed today
you sit there and count yours
not the number but the kind
let's shy away from glee mechanical:

the corporate laugh that blurs the whine of tedium
the social yuck that wheezes small despair
we'll toss these out and screw false grins down tight
what we're seeking: soulful, hearty chuckling.

The kind that breaks from deep down in the guttural
flings us tearful from the church 'cause we can't stop
trips us rolling down the germy office floor,
pushes us toward managers with resignations.

Kind laughter of a universe that won't stop trying,
that bubbles up within warfare's delusion
the spacious chortle pleasing, never wounding
that's what I'm looking for and seldom find.

There's snicker clubs that say they practice yoga
they force a giggle, grin, they laugh "as if"
sometimes that works, no fooling, real laughter
sometimes it catches in our modern throat.

I say laughter shows the real God's presence
jokes prove we're more than accidental slime
throw back your head and guffaw if you're able
you're soloist in heaven's raucous choir.

If I Knew

So little time, and if I knew
I would rush out into streets and alleys,
down to the sunny marsh
to watch herons fish.

I would take up with the neighborhood,
make acquaintance with the Labrador
who barks in the yard and needs a walk
and I would offer to walk him.

I would call you up, and say let's meet
and talk about everything
let's meet before the sun goes down
drink cups of delicious coffee

get to know each other again
before I take off on my spring bicycle
whose tires I have just pumped up
and I'd ride hands-free like a child.

And if I knew how little time
I'd lie in bed with her the whole evening
after a crispy salad and vegetable lasagna
and we would watch the late show, chuckle, and fall asleep.

I would wake in the early dark morning
kneel by the window, listen for the train's horn
as it hauls freight from mysterious Indiana
and the night moon still rides high.

I would do these things, I would
celebrate the very sidewalks,
I would call out to all the world
love this, love me, there is so little time.

So What? Here's What!

So what if you don't appreciate conceptual art?
so what if you find poetry gibberish,
you to-do-list during the classical concert
and ballet leaves your body icy cold?

You're crook-faced, your frame's askew
you find no thrills in professional football
you were a B minus student
and most of the time you want to be alone.

Comparisons are fatal
yet you spend your wounded life making them,
overlooking your glorious achievement
your honorable, eccentric pastimes.

Why not blast through to the peaceful center
loll in your mouth the words you cherish
romp with the passing basset you adore
drag cranky felines back into your life.

We all act as chief critic of our days
so we spend our lives in miserable reflection
instead of striking out among the dandelions,
following the flight of the blue heron.

Relax in the true comfort of your spirit's life
where you grow, and no one is accusing
put aside loss, gain, overweening emotion
surrender to what's before you, in you, now.

That's all there is, anyway, your beauty
your perfection shouts out to the whole universe
but your ears are stopped, you cannot hear
so you sink into the illusion of imperfection.

50   I hope you find the sun within you
I hope you turn your compassionate gaze upon yourself
I wish you happiness, fun, and, absolutely, pleasure
most of all peace, in the long light here and hereafter.

Trouble

I meet an old-time farmer from Salem, Oregon,
says he's been working organic for thirty years
former English teacher, former wordsmith,
he tells me he names all his cows.

Says he calls one "Sausage," another "Steaks"
says he tells them every day he'll kill them
gets them easy and accustomed, he declares,
they know one day they're gonna die.

I ask him how do you kill, kill humanely?
He says, I murder clean, they never know the truth.
How? I ask, and he flaunts a .22 pistol
there's a certain "X" that marks the spot, he claims,

between the open eye, the open ear
and I talk sweet to them, he says, like always
I say good morning, croon of succulent pastures
then I aim real close and straight, then I pull the trigger.

They quick sink down to their knees, he says,
fall forward, no pain, no knowledge
maybe I'd like to die like that, I say
maybe I could manage that, he says.

Next day I meet his young homesteader neighbor
struggling to sow and reap and pay the bills.
You know old Jack and his .22? I ask.
He replies, did Jack tell you about his chicken?

Old Jack, he says, keeps hens for meager laying,
one's named "Trouble," 'cause she always flies the coop
lays her eggs on the front door stoop, or in the pickup bed
nothing but trouble, Jack says, then one day he kills her.

Had to, he says, she stopped laying, kept on eating
wrung her neck, says he, far from the coop
where Fryer, Broiler, and Drumstick wouldn't see it.
Ounce of pity, I reply, in a heart so cold.

Jack didn't hardly speak for a day, the young farmer says,
couldn't, he was swallowing all his tears.
Next time I see Jack, I say, I'll ask him:
Why is everything so much trouble?

Why?

Why did you choose to smile
at the very moment the cat came crying for dinner
and the couple across the street
were hanging out Christmas lights
on an early November afternoon
and the woman laughed heartily, chokingly, at
her slender husband's cavorting, his homely
cartwheels, and he said something rude and funny
I couldn't quite make out as a yellow 1989
Corolla came bumping down the street
and a late autumn maple at just that instant
flung her leaves downward onto the sidewalk
and a wind rustled lavender stalks
in our impermanent backyard garden, just so,
as somebody turned on a radio for the Ohio State
football game, and I caught the second half of
a broadcast syllable in the quiet afternoon,
and tell me, then, why, at that precise moment,
did you choose to smile?

Daemon

Whatever happened to that old devil fun
skipping through the meadow with friendly mutts,
lazing back on green grass, wide-eyed at blue sky,
encircled by buzzing planes on high?

Fording Ellicott Creek, trapping minnows
in pools where they blindly swam,
clamping on roller skates, roaring down
Blantyre Road straight toward the ice cream man.

Now it's obligation and the office
now I "contribute to the community"
raise my hand, say something useful,
write down wise words to be applauded.

But beagles slink away when I approach
afternoon movies close their doors to me
the skateboard broke in half in the garage
and Ellicott Creek is dry.

I wouldn't know where to run
to find my fun that sauntered away
I see him capering in the distance
I'll never catch him.

I want to eat chocolate, not exercise
write poems that poets don't like
slump in front of cable TV
dream away in the garden bower.

Don't want to send obligatory e-mails
don't want to meet the chairman of the department,
nod my head at the pork producers' conference,
read the serious New York literature I ought to.

I want to dress up like a banshee
spook out lovers in the park
perform night ceremonies honoring witches
spread my cape, sprout wings, and fly.

I don't know where my soul went
he's abandoned the conversation
I've left him on the precipice
we're both about to fall off.

Give me a shot of the whiskey of life
I'll drink it down till I'm past cold sober
hope I can see a gamboling horizon
before lights snap out and my spirit is extinguished.

Healer

She was a healer
with strong healing hands
her eyes were like a clear night sky
her body was rooted in the earth
she was an old tree
she was rock and crystal
she was a healer.

He was a young man
fear held him in its tight arms
and he was an old man
he needed a healing.

Far away his mother sang to him
somewhere he could not see her
the old healer found her
and took her up in loving arms
and held her
and rocked her gently.

Soon his mother quieted
soon his mother slept
he was ready for a healing
he was ready for a wholeness
when he saw his mother sleeping
he knew the time was ready.

The old woman
crooning over him and breathing
he thought she was a witch
and then he thought she was a sailor
his body was a ship
his blood it was the ocean
she held crystals in the fading light

her hands were warm against him
and with her healing touch
his bonds were loosed and broken.

His mother she lay dreaming
in the quiet sleep of peace
through the years and all the ages
her soul was white and rested
he knelt beside her
he kissed her gently
and then she let him go.

He was flying into a great light
the old healer, like a father
was there to guide him
the light blazed and shone
it covered him
it burned him clean.

When he awoke
she sat beside him, smiling
she handed him a crystal
old woman handed him her words
he handed her his life
and then he handed her his dreams
and when the fair exchange was done
she kissed him at the door
she gave to him a gift
a present with a ribbon
which he opened at the highway.

It was his dreams
it was his body and his blood
it was his pure spirit shining.

Conscientious Defector

To save the fern I've got to kill
those bugs that they call "scale"
a minor soak of alcohol
will end their brief travail.

To prance across the lawn, I fear
will end some insect lives
I do not wish them any harm
I'll shoo them to their hives.

I fear we're all pale killers
efficient with our thrust
and though we might be vegan
were eating more than dust.

This plant that I am chewing
as I rend doth scream
again, I'm merely living,
nonviolence a dream.

I'd like to be a pussycat
but then I'd rip up mouses
or a giant ape in Borneo
but then I'd dine on louses.

A peaceful man I am, for sure
I'd never harm a vector
I have no overwhelming need
to grab a rat, dissect 'er.

But if I try to live my life
I've truly got to murder
please tell me God, what I should do
this couldn't wax absurder.

To a Sour Lover

Let us meander happy through the day
not touching upon the afternoon's worries
like the tiny bee lighting upon the spike.
Let's put aside complaint and grieving.

Since you and I share time, are not immortal
why can't we conjure a near-perfect hour
of joy, enchantment, chorusing laughter,
intertwined with caring and compassion.

Do not torment me with pale discourse
about the harsh sigh of life you comprehend
your memories of lack and imperfection
your exhalation of mortality's affliction.

We will have moment enough for sorrow
now we can stroll the day unspecifying
sip the wine of pleasure, incomprehension
rest in each others' arms as darkness falls.

Prate not of corporeal troubles
our morning air is sweetly scented
cool water lies just beyond the hill
the meadowlark trills in the linden tree.

Let us fashion our season of contentment
pleasing in both light and shade
there is so little time for grand enjoyment
make haste, the sun burns on his way.

Tick-tock

Just when your day is set minute for minute
your spouse inconvenient says: let's stop at Krogers
just when you'd figured a march to the parkway
would leave time to study, then rush to the gym.

All right, you say, as you feel your watch throbbing
meet you, self-checkout, exactly two minutes
but nobody knows where the pita bread molders
you're falling behind in your runaway day.

Swift you get home, you resolve to skip lunching
sprint up to your office, attend moods creative
but you glance at the lid of your groaning computer
there's blood and detritus, the cat has been sunning.

He's bleeding from who knows where, maybe a foot
so you've gotta find him, examine his toes
mad clocks are chiming, gym doors will be closing
your task opportunities wither away.

Your digital watch is declaring, reminding
you might have forgotten an afternoon meeting
as you drag cat complaining from under the table
his claws catch and hold in your new flannel shirt.

After you've checked him (the cat's quite OK)
your treadmill desire is unsuitably fading
maybe you'd just like to read for a while
watch the sun dip into mid-winter dark.

That's not the energy you would have wanted
the regimentation that's captured your way
your time's running out on this organized day
and there's so little you have accomplished.

Why not defer to the casual universe
why not relax into this-instant pleasure
dangle your watch in a bubbling bathtub
grin as the shattering numbers fade.

Your life's not accomplishment, nor productivity
no one recalls your awards at your wake
your headstone is mute on degrees, papers published
there's one memory of your life that remains:

a person humane or a son of a bitch
the mourners will speak as they file from the grave
as Huxley once said, try to be a bit kinder
their last fading image: your tenderness, babe.

Buyer's Market

There's a yard sale around the corner
on this August afternoon, mostly junk,
but I bought a retractable phone cord
for a dollar, maybe it'll work.

This guy with a Willie Nelson voice
is tending the sale at his girlfriend's house.
Says he works at Mike's Barber Shop, the janitor.
Says: " We're gettin' outta Dodge."

Stepping up, a plaintive girlfriend voice:
"I need you to bring out those CDs."
As he passes me: "This guy wants to buy a phone cord."
"He's driving me crazy," confides the droopy-faced woman.

Well, we're all just trying to get by, aren't we?
It's a sunny day, nothing much moving but maples in the breezes
a calming Sunday, everything on the lawn priced to sell,
these folks are driving out somewhere, Kansas or California.

There's everything relaxed about the orange cat
who rubs against my hand, flanks shaven, me skittish.
"He's yours?" I ask. "No, crazy cat lady next door."
There's an elemental quiet and complicity here

complicity in the loose-limbed afternoon
when just for a moment, all judgments dissolve:
suspicions between janitor and poet,
exasperations of his worn-out girl friend.

It's a calm afternoon we're sharing together
we don't need any interfering brain-storms
for a little while we can all make out:
the priced-to-sell yard sale gets one of my dollars

the frustrated lady gets to say a sincere thank you
the man-janitor gets to ease, "Why not two, a dollar fifty?"
And "That's Jerry Garcia, driving that truck on by."
We can all be temporarily grateful for the day and each other's presence.

I'd like to pass a sale like this every weekend
the eternal yard sale on Ventura Street in Columbus, Ohio
where you get to lay down your burden for a few minutes
and buy something cheap and practical, besides.

You Always Have an Answer

When I say:
I think God visited me in a dream last night
you say: So what was it you ate for dinner?

When I say:
I think that God may have a perfect love for you and me
you say: Wishful thinking.

When I say:
My grandfather spoke to me from heaven
you say: That was your brain chemistry talking.

And when I say:
Maybe, just maybe, we'll have life eternal
you say: Where's your evidence?

I've heard your answers for so long now
I think they must come from a broken heart
come sit with me for a while
let us put aside all these questions, these opinions.

Maybe infinite love will touch us
maybe in silence He will cherish us
maybe there will be no more need for
my doubt, your certitude, our terrible loss.

If

If all our hearts are rocks and bones
if all our souls are paper stuffed with twigs
then hands I offer you are nerves and gases,
dark liquids, snapping leathers, pale ivory.
The glow within your eyes is fire electric
the words that leave your mouth,
the sighs of tissues scraping.

The stars and whirling suns beyond are dumb
the animal that creeps is wound with springs
your spirit love, your loyalty
are movements of the wind
that shudders roughly over earth
pushed slow by wheels of iron.

Then all the lives that linger in the darkness
or lives that flame and dance with power bright
they end the same, unseen and heard but briefly
all around the dim and failing light.

So What's Up?

Buddhists tell me I'll become the cosmos
some yak-related say I'll be a whale
my Jewish friends, they say we cease forever
finally, I'm groping in a fog.

I have a Christian friend who says I'm damned
that God elected me for hellish torture
a sweet guy, but his sanity's in question
he says he'll pray for me, but no thanks, pal.

Maybe some accept annihilation
maybe they've no grief about their doom
but I would love to know I'm loved eternal
in my theology, death finds no room.

My atheist friends, they tell me I'm deluded
my Muslim friends say I should kiss their book
my Baptist friends say Jesus is the way
my head is spinning, so I'll hit the road.

I'll ask the universe for indications
that I am treasured far beyond all thought
I'll free my mind of anger, conflagration,
let kindness be my hallmark in this life.

Maybe I will learn, direct and certain
that I will live in God's eternal peace
that He is not a being of fear or vengeance
that love, in fact, does truly conquer all.

If I'm misguided, maybe that's my fate
if I'm naïve, then maybe that's my faith
I'm placing reason in a smaller basket
searching in the quiet for signs and signals.

Like St. Theresa, Rumi, gentle Francis
I'll strike out on a journey of my heart
I'm hoping I will find a loving Partner
to touch my soul, to cherish my small life.

To My Walking Pneumonia

You grabbed me by the chest and sloughed me off
infected buoyant life with your distress
left me with a lung that wouldn't breathe
coughed me up through many sleepless dreams.

How did you distract my deep defense
discover flaws in my corpuscle armor?
You sailed right past me on my mucous sea
I didn't get a chance to get a grip.

You left me with no hankering for life
struck me sleeping all day in the parlor
wouldn't let me share sweet spring's commencement
downed me with a fever when I bitched.

It took a brutal pill to kill you off
the one I aimed directly at your throat
one final choking retch, you failed away
I thought you'd left me free to repossess.

But though you've gone, my body newly craves
the relaxation you so firm commanded
I lie about the bed, no motivation
no energy to muse or care or fret.

But that's the gift you gave me after all
the rest that let me know that I need nada
that I don't have to drudge, produce or act
that me abed is wondrous, nothing less.

Biding Time

All time different:
love-making time
different from torture time
different from popcorn time.

Hemlock tree has greening time
river rat, nest-building time
blue heron, focused fishing time
me, self-flagellation time.

Hours not hours at all
that's what we call the clock
some minutes are the whole afternoon
plying balmy summer sidewalks.

I'll seep into the river rat's body
for one patient and industrious morning
sit in the cranium of the heron
swim the eye of a drowsing tom

because I'm doing prison time
I'm in four-walled jail time
bouncing around my bone-dead skull
can't break out for a casual smoke.

Cut me a temporary prefrontal lobotomy.
I'll cook my breakfast in the hut of the spirit
in the time-loose forest of the living
and the resurrected dead.

O! H! I! O!

Right in the middle of October snarl and storm
this giant-limbed guy, girlfriend compact, sturdy
are laughing like it's easy September,
charging along the slick walks to the Ohio State game.

Most everybody else is sulking indoors
moaning about hibernal throes 30 days early
I ponder the differences in how we capture living:
clamped down tight and morbid, or leaping in the day.

Won't give this conundrum too much notice
just enough to know my possibility
for happy outdoor bundling up on a rainy afternoon
instead of a chilled-down, couch-filled TV death watch.

I wonder if that couple is sparkling, clean and bright
buffered in the blear loud throng-filled stadium
I'll bet they're joyous, no scarlet and gray beers
I'll bet they're in or out of love, celebratory.

I'll hold them in mind as I hunch on down to the Kroger's
cursing the inconvenient home game Chevy traffic
they're my gleaming example, my Midwest lodestar
lighting up the dark seas of my fogged Columbus desire.

Life's a ... 71

Just when you're getting it all together, said Pete Seeger,
it's time to die, then he strummed into song, *Climbing
Jacob's Ladder,* I think. Well, Pete's not dead yet,
and I don't know whether he's ever got beyond the first few rungs.

I haven't for sure, and I don't know when I'll bite the mat
but this stormy winter day in April makes me feel
I could capsize anytime, and that's accurate,
that's what old Father Carnahan at St. Teresa's in Bangor says.

He says we do not know the hour or the day
and death comes like a thief in the night and I wonder
why all his parishioners keep coming back to hear
inspirational crap like that, that couldn't help but make them feel
good.

But I have to credit the geezer, as I depart the church and spy
a used condom on the vestibule floor, he does have a point there,
in the sermon, I mean, not the condom, every spring morning
could be our last and why do we struggle so hard

to make each moment better for ourselves, happiness so elusive.
I like that elder Buddha Thich Nhat Hanh who, I heard, strolls
down the block hugging every tree like it's an ecstatic moment
and wouldn't I like to walk that way but twenty years of meditation

haven't trimmed my foul outlook and branches just keep
getting in the way, and I can't remember the last time
I clutched any one of them exalted. My friend Shelley in Buffalo
says the cliché is true: "Life's a bitch and then you die."

A cheap thrust here could be, "Yeah, that *would* be true in Buffalo."
But I know better: I know life's a bitch, then it's a thrill and maybe
more thrilling for those well-endowed with pleasure optimizers,
anchored in a more fortunate brain chemistry that repeatedly

shocks them happy as they prance down the tree-rimmed lane
and some days I feel like hugging those oaks and willows, some days
like axing them down, chopping mercilessly, so I guess I'm
human just like you, and today I have no better answers, sorry.

Joy to the World 73

Outdoorsmen in Maine are yelling for snow
on Great Plains they're pleading: desist, enough!
But aren't we, all of us, sent here to savor
warm winter cocoa, and keen ice for skating?

We're here in delight, our capacity varied
morbid or sunny, we'll forge a glad hour
the universe hastened the Big Bang on forward
to sunny New Hampshire, Ohio-bright seasons

where little Maurice slides on neighborhood ice,
the elderly Goldsteins ski frozen rivers,
they all can tolerate dark clouds alighting
if they can limber their icicle bones

on once-green spring earth, now blear-frosty,
plus winter-day blockbusters unspool to see,
hot soup for kids fresh from frost-bitten ranging
Hemingway, Zane Grey to read by the fire.

Isn't all life a creative unfolding?
and sure there'll be trial and heartache arriving
but courage as well, all angelic support
while winter wind quickens your wandering skis.

Don't tell me that all life is drear anxious suffering.
Weren't we created to have a good time?
Christians vote four-star the deep Peace of Christ
Hindus — Namaste! — behold God in you.

Surely the Deity, shapely or formless
can't be a dour and dithering monarch
so undulate happily, cultivate joy
there's monsters enough approaching our climes.

We can do, we can be, we can love, we can serve
elements all of hibernal eternal
we'll leap, we'll dance, we'll shout or inscribe
this divine moment is ours for devouring.

Shame on You?

How could you feel sour and dejected
when the world somersaults chuckling around you
when the winter moon is lovely on hushed snowfall
when your body tells you it's ready to hopscotch away.

How could you favor this term of no endearment
when the Creator has granted you the necessities of joy
when all about you flails multifarious bliss opportunity
who are you to push it ungratefully away?

I'll tell you who you are to do that:
you're a being capable of sorrows and depths
you don't need to wallow in small despairs,
but you're sure entitled to know they're OK.

Whoever said happiness is steady and constant?
Fifty gray successive winter skies melt it away.
You're entitled to burrow deep inside yourself
pack your bags, step in, depart the day.

No, I'm not telling you to cultivate unhappiness
or amplify obscure, indecent grudges
but you have a right to know a secret:
feeling bad for an hour or week is perfectly great.

Don't fly away into false unruliness
addictions can magnify an angry thrust
you don't want to supersize your dejection
by growing it through repetitive ways.

But your life unique is messy, inconstant
just a chemical low can tear apart your day
so don't hope for a light that's not appearing soon
dive down your unhappiness: for a while, suffer away.

Eclipsed
for Perkins Observatory Director Tom Burns

Very late tonight our planet's shadow
will pass across the mountains of the moon
they're all awake, those Wesleyan star trackers
they're locked inside their telescopic night.

They're led by a fanatic who digresses
who teaches stars to children ripped from Wii's
who blathers on about the constellations
who finds a mystery in winter's skies.

But here I lie amused on brimming Facebook
my iPad takes me where I want to go
it shows me shifting maps of pixeled stars
devised by programmed man, as if I care.

The passing stars no longer captivate me
when lighted Walmart stupefies my needs
and I can stroll to my pre-heated Prius
that won't besmirch this ivory season's air.

Who knows the stars of bold Orion's sword
who cares to hear his ancient hunter story
and sparkling Draco Dragon disappeared
when dragons ceased to roam the fabled earth.

We're far advanced from need to watch the night
our winter wants are met by Chinese toilers
unlucky stars, neglected earth discarded
we, all of us, are happy manufactured.

About Face

Here's a day to feel sleepy, cozy
rolled up loose in the rug of indolence
falling away softly from the hurried,
cables uprooted and dangling.

Time blooms open, barely moves
no finger writing on any page
you can feel the weeping in your body
the calm in your unfurling mind.

No deals today for extrovert striving
transmitters silenced, lines are dead
even the petulant self is muted,
that grim conversation has drifted away.

On a pyre, we are burning invitations
to a thousand thousand revelries
the envelopes are scattered
the pen is dry of chattering ink.

It will be like a day in youth's summer
when the long sun lighted the campus green
the buildings of ivied stone lingered
the hearty hound running and happily running.

Fear creeps away down a dim corridor
your body slips into a wakeful dream
you cannot recall the equation, the brutish formula
you hold yourself in your own lengthening arms.

"Stop!" the longtime cry, the gainless wailing
at last stilled by your quenched and dying ambition
and all the heavens are singing and singing
this hymn of a strong and silent retreating.

Measure Up!

Dead rank tired and wonky slumberous
summertime lethargy beats you down to bed
maybe a shot of Industrial Cola®
would vault you up productive.

The unspoken meaning behind the word:
you do and do, from Pulitzer to laundry
never go fishing, drop a line, no hook,
nor lend the hour to solitude and dreaming.

Push on through your fatigue, your painful dally
mount a check list, the day's end accomplished
no good musing over the blooming summer lawn:
rip it, cut it, tame it beyond compassion.

Each day is valued by what have you done
a hundred projects balanced on your globe
that's how you feel good, mighty in the world
that's how you're better than nothing at all.

Do, do, do what your heart won't
analyze, order, quantify, build
haul out the yardstick of comparison
stack yourself up beside it.

It's not the happy moment that gives life meaning
it's projects, plans, frenzy, data
no time for sadness, anxiety's a waste
you're productive? they'll pat your glowing shoulder.

Cast aside leisurely lazing and drowsing
the martinet clock is the measure of your mean
judge yourself, rank yourself, good time for sergeants
salute yourself only if you've quantified your dreams.

Born-again

You used to be the boy who forged the cattail swamps
you netted the monarch, stroked her fine wings,
rode high on your bicycle out to Ellicott Creek
plunged down heedless into muddy waters.

You were the imp who shouted in the St. Rose church
the monster who plagued Love's delicatessen
you shrieked down the alleyway, daring the sky come get you,
taunted red-eyed devils in the evening bushes.

But here you are, struck down with disappointment
you hold up the globe like a burden instead of a balloon
your brain is a homing device probing the earth for worries
you ignite, you stoke each personal conflagration.

Once you wandered free with summer zephyrs
clambered aboard boxcars, caroling into distances
you chortled when people told you life was brief
you drank a deep Orange Crush and threw the bottle away.

How did you become the one who calculates the hours,
who fosters every care in a world you once deemed careless?
How do we find you, anoint you with your holy birthright?
Deliver us your sorrows, beg us heal you, we'll lead the way.

Look! Spiders are beckoning, herons are winging
dandelions have thrust up golden to please you
this whole August day is wanting your sultry company
the evening will tempt you with her many fragrances.

Come go with us down to the river of time,
to your long-discarded innocence, your tossed-aside freedoms
you can live with us, a boy among sheltering willows
by the water's edge we'll consecrate, we'll bless your new-born way.

Let's Get Mad

Let's all get mad together
let's gin up some grievance and yell
you can find a reason to grind
search your mind, you'll find an irritant.

We'll form a circle
we'll hold hands together
at the signal of a blessing
we'll give an angry shout.

We'll scream till we're a little hoarse,
but save some force for personal time
you get to tell us who you're pissed at,
how long you've been holding your outrage in.

Rehearse all your arguments
how the offender is in the wrong
then speak them out slowly
savor each accusation.

Bring along a blood pressure meter
we don't want you up in stroke territory
the idea here: give vent to healthy rage
the idea here: blame whoever you can.

Then comes along part two of getting angry
you don't have to stay for this
it takes a little courage:
we'll speak the sorrow beneath your ire.

How the transgressor hurt your heart
how you felt small when you heard his cutting words
how he reminds you of your elderly uncle
the one you wouldn't see before he died.

It's OK to cry a little
your tears are encouraged to flow
we'll hold hands around our circle
and comfort one another.

Then comes along part three of getting mad
a lot of people leave before this one
here we move beneath the hurt and shame and sorrow
to find deep peace inside us, there all along.

It takes a bit of time, to feel within,
a willingness to let both sorrow and anger go
but if you can stay for the whole of our meeting today
you'll find a healing quiet you can reach lifelong.

Your Day

Tell me about your disheartening, your travail,
the grief you discovered in your hollowed shoulders,
how your soul's creativity no longer pleases you
I'll listen carefully, however long you speak.

I won't be smug in my receiving of your sorrow
I understand you need a friendly hand on your shoulder
you might need to cry in my arms and that's OK
if I'm judgmental, it won't be about you, not today.

You can tell me everything that's disappointed you
your wish you had lived another life in another place.
You can let me know, with safety, that you'd really rather be
someone else, someone that you, your chief critic, approves of.

You can relax today and feel your sadness
no need to reach for a cigarette, for television, or sex
you can take this day to learn how much you hurt
how you feel abandoned by your own heart.

We'll talk it out, you'll feel it through, time is limitless right now
then, when you're ready to go, I hope you've felt some relief.
We all need a day to contact our deep sorrows.
One day I'll knock at your door. Please answer. It will be my day.

Winter Instant

There they were, leaping out before him:
snow-clutched trees, howling automobiles, delicate sparrows
and, marvel of all, cascading down the icy street, a man,
wool cap down over his eyes, determined by his mind and headed somewhere.

In that moment everything sprang forward
they cried out, "Look at us!" and
he saw them all with his heart's eye
for a fleeting moment before he slept.
As though intensity would overcome him
he closed his eyes and drifted into fantasies.

Dream monsters appeared, products of his time and memory
unpleasantness abounded, incoherent strife assailed him
but it was finally sleep and restful, he overcame his anxious inheritance,
then swam his way awake and the world poured back into view.

How could he have missed it, that red-capped man, those snow-branched
beeches, resting here in front of him, calling out to him:
notice us, be with us, share in our everlasting glory,
and for a moment he did, vibrant there among them.

He saw all things as a benign creation: the bawling autos,
jabbering crows, oil-muddied snow tracks, slim jet contrail,
his own burbling stomach, the sharp stabbing of his left ankle
mingled together in a shimmering instant.

He tried to grasp them up and bring them in the house
which had its own bubble and shine
for a while he had them, and he held them
all together in a sprawling ecstasy

which faded away over dinner and the paying of bills
vanished in the lure of the computer
but within he knew that each machine, each pressure of pen,
the steaming soup and the mutton lamb held it all before him,
through him and with him and in him the spirit gloried
and sometimes, he knew, he would notice, participate, and rejoice.

Stop. Please.

Don't give me any awards
don't send any opportunities my way
stop every unceasing demand
just stay away from me.

Don't tell me I've got the greatest talents
don't call me into any meeting
if you need help today
some other stooge might be available.

This is the way I want it:
I want to sit and stare at the blossoming tulip tree
and maybe I'll journey into her deep branches.
I don't want to be judged about that, either.

Go away and leave me alone
sell my car to the Kidney Foundation
I'm not driving anywhere, no obligations
and don't ask me to make excuses, either.

I've mastered the craft of disappearing,
shut down my e-mail, switched off my cell
I'm jumping on my bicycle and pedaling
down along the river that flows forever away.

I hope you won't come after me with pleadings
I trust you'll abide by my separation directive
but if you don't, I'm cycling a hidden trail
and you won't find me with your infinite GPS search.

Hang up your regard for me
don't be concerned about my being friendless
I'm dead and I like it that way,
don't need you to resurrect me.

86 Maybe some day you'll get a phone call
when you're at lunch, I'll commune with your voice mail
I'll tell you I'm doing fine, tell you I love you.
Thank God and technology you can't trace the call.

Counseling Our Youth

I will champion you till my expiration, your sometimes
decision to contact your spirit, nevermind the irrelevant other,
those stray activities, so enticing, that do not nourish,
everything cross-thread, those hours you drink from a polluted glass,

within you a combat pushing you to pursuits other than gladness,
compulsion and desire of a young lifetime of embarrassment,
sorrowful the shame and discord within, and it is yours the same as mine
once more the lesson of the soul to learn, the deep happiness

and yes the thrill, and yes I like the word, excitement,
at the very center of your brief existence that chord is played
and beyond that you cannot claim for yourself anything but
the dead repetition of stylized thought and performance.

How long before, spirit cast aside, you reach a knowing of
your single self, first teacher, who walks beside you and waits,
beseeching you silently to cherish your high calling
which is joyful, spontaneous, serious, never long-faced.

When will you relax into the being you were intended,
no fear governing, no hesitation over the vamp of a careering society
you have only to follow the certain course you truly know
it is touching you, like your fingers touch the pleasantness of morning.

When will you greet the one you love and understand
when will you grant yourself your own forgiveness
soaring above the demands of the various, touching down home
every moment, no doubt, no reason to anything other than prevail.

That's Life/Death?

When the cat you love lies dying
when you win that award for productivity
when you're bored with mundane work
when you can't figure out your calling

when you have the happiest marriage in the world
but you know you could die at any moment
when you're headed for your PhD
and you'll make it without jumping off the tower:

could it be that this is what your life is?
This mundane, sad, happy, messy stuff
things that go wrong or right for you
all the emotional swings and harrowings?

But if that's what life is all about
what about death, what's that?
the end to all your mental burble?
finis to all your virtues and crimes?

Maybe a reward and after-life
maybe a God who loves you after all
a heaven where your family meets you at the gate
eternal bliss in a loving presence.

Some say the grave's the end, that you're erased
"rolled round the earth with rocks and stones and trees"
your jellied brain fodder for the worms
your atoms scattered in the dung of sheep.

Now there would be a cosmic joke: you're gone,
created toward your own annihilation
everything you've planned and gained, everyone you love
departed from your memory and you, long-term, from theirs.

I'd like to think that Christian Merton guy
who plumbed the Buddhist mind and meditated
had it right that God loves you and me,
confirmed His presence in our thankful hearts.

Maybe if we take that as a premise
swallow reason's pride and act "as if"
we'll tune to something deep within our spirit
that brings us peace and kindness every day.

So we can hope, though Zen folk say we shouldn't,
that we are loved eternal, past our family
that we are in His hands each slim-cord moment
that guardian spirits help us in our days.

So when death phones and we can't argue
we'll know we lived a life of joy and justice
ready for a hand-grasp through the veil,
for our good and faithful servant entrance.

Pause

When we halt our inner converse
the universe is still, like a bold
mouse pausing, not to be espied.
When our monologue ceases

our earth is quiet like sunlight
drifting through afternoon lace
like the distant sigh of an old furnace,
the murmur of leaves in spring wind.

Cacophonous our mind's production
uproarious the raving day within
until we pause to recover
our whole, calm spirit.

Clear the evening angelus bell
hushed the noonday train yard
soft the parlor cat sleeping
bright the air in deepest woods.

This our harmony
this our own cathedral
we err to leave it for the mind outrageous
we could live our lives in sacred dwelling.

Departures

God's Loss

When your spirit left the world, God's playtime was hindered
he can't find that certain way of laughing anymore
he won't know that playful touch on the shoulder
that huge grin that caused young men to stumble.

He won't hear love professed anymore, not the way you did
won't share your delight over new tomatoes in the garden
nor will he know the impatience that brought you to tears
or feel the night dreams startling you awake.

God won't hold a babe in his arms, not the way you could
or say goodbye to your son, his own, at the door.
There'll be no morning coffee on your cool terrace
not for him, he'll need to journey elsewhere.

He'll miss the happy tangle of your first spring kite-flying,
the way you saw the sun declining and applauded the day.
Poor God, he couldn't know your death would mean for him
this loneliness, this loss that all of heaven cannot replace.

Wings

Over the river hangs a mist
and on the river
a single gray Canada goose.
You can see him in the mist
swimming in fast circles
looking for his mate, calling her.

He has crossed the river
east and west
for hours now
and she does not appear.

He stops and eats
standing by the water's edge
but as he eats he listens
for her familiar cry.
He is alone at the river and waiting.

Now night by the river
begins to fall
and still he cannot find her.
He swims more quickly now
thrusting at the water
with powerful strokes
he calls more often and more loudly
but all the river is silent.

The darkness falls; he waits and watches
his animal eyes see by the moon
watching for a flicker of wings
searching for her dark body against the water
he does not sleep, he moves but slowly
and so he passes the night.

He is on the river as the sun rises
he is there and calling as the mist clears
and when she does not come
he knows that she is gone forever.

Silently his great wings
carry him toward the sky
he circles, far above the water, twice
he calls once more, so clear and loudly
and then he flies and flies.

His eyes are toward the north
his body moves with the wind
the river shines in the sunlight
below him and behind him.

Death Uncomprehended

I don't *get* Death, I don't understand him
how casual he is, as he picks us off:
a plane crash, a fall down stairs,
an organ's slow collapse, a gunshot.

There's nothing elegant about his choices
he's no aesthete, this destroyer of our worlds
he doesn't ask permission, no courtesies in our leaving
our loved ones hear the news on the telephone.

I'd ask him for a painless departure
if I could find him, somewhere beyond the veil
but he's horrifically busy, even weekends,
flitting about the cosmos, he's after numbers.

I wish I could say he shows a dollop of mercy
but I think he's instinctual, like a hawk
snatching a mouse up out of a field
ripping it apart with relish, eating to survive.

If we were given life eternal, I don't know what he'd do
God won't play backgammon with him
he has nothing in common with the Creator anyway
he's on his own with his bounty hunter's license.

So I see us all dissolving into sorrow
as death carries our loved ones away
and finally, our passing nears, no defenses,
we crouch and fear the darkness overtaking.

I hope you have a good rapport with Death,
perhaps you're ready to take his hand and follow
maybe you have no problem with his methods,
you'll float peacefully into the sad beyond.

I'll try to trick him and outrun him
I'll hide when he approaches my door
I know in the end he'll add me to his scrapbook
but I'll fight and flee, I'll grant him power, nothing more.

When My Father Died

When my father died
angels were in the church
I could see their whiteness
everywhere
I could feel the fanning
of their wings
as I rose and walked
to the altar
to read the final blessing.

There are those who say
there were no angels present
that at the graveyard
there was only the warm autumn air
the few old friends
the stolid gravediggers.

But I saw them
I saw them standing in tribute
to their old companion
they were on all sides
they spoke of my father's life
with honor, with respect.

When the coffin was lowered
I didn't watch
but if I had
I would have seen
the white angels
my father with them
leaving the clumsy body
entering the kingdom of the spirit
comforted, strong, and unafraid.

When I Go

When I go, I go, that's all
it might be on a windswept morning
or in gloom and deep of winter
or on a scented, lovely day.

I'll disappear, and you will cry,
I do not choose this leaving
but now I feel I can accept
the end of my travail.

It could be on a moonstruck night
in spring when all the world's aborning
or over breakfast, tea and toast,
or putting on one pantleg.

I might look silly when I fail,
or I might leave dramatic
crushed by highway trucks a-flaming,
dropping down from shearing skies.

I'll end in peace or end in pain
today or at my century
when I go, I'll know your face,
heaven's power cannot erase.

I'll hope we meet again someday
just like that pop song says
and I'll extend my hand to you
when you approach the bridge.

But I know that we will end
and that's OK with me
because I have convinced myself
we'll love eternally ... maybe.

Fisherman Eternal

The fisherman standing in the stream
is surrounded by the whole world,
and you watching with me are leaving
and I am leaving you.

Slowly, at first, none would notice
but gradually we fail
and that whole world is telling us
to take the time to go.

The world is waving goodbye to us
the river rat patiently building her nest
the bright geese drowsing on the banks
the woodpecker cheerfully knocking at the elm

and all the children who accompanied us
with their lively laughter uplifting us.
There were times when the world grew pale
and the terrible pain seemed unending

but all that sorrow is leaving
it seems now like the trouble of an instant
and we remember happily, gratefully,
time having eased our memories.

The smiling world is telling us
to pack our bags for another place
she calls out our destination
she announces the stop and the station.

And sometimes we hear her
when our spirits are rested and quiet
we understand the journey required
though we may not tell our selves.

100

The fisherman casts a long green line
it whistles over the water
the clear sky snaps with energy
the river trees sing in a southern wind.

We hold each other's hands, surrounded
by the glistening, tranquil day
and the goodbye we are saying
is also hello and arrival.

The Death Interviews

I ask marauding Death if he provides
sense beyond the body putrefied
he replies obliquely, "We shall see."
I fear he may seek merely to torment me.

I batter him with every angled logic
thinking I'll befuddle him with brilliance
trick a revelation of his sprawling domain
discover if it's fantasy or real.

I offer sheaves of reasoned argument
he spurns my syllogistic manufactures
I call them out, pursuing down his corridor
he wheels around, politely yawns, then vanishes.

I strive to conquer him in Bergman chess
hope he'll spill the beans, his king a captive
he sweeps my knights aggressive off the board
and glowering, departs into his mist.

He always trails a mist along behind him
left over from an antique horror movie
apparently he feels a need of stagecraft
to mystify, to escalate my anguish.

But I'd just like him to be straight with me:
Heaven's realm, or swift annihilation?
Burning hell or consciousness departed?
Perhaps it's not his job to educate.

I guess he works at God's eternal pleasure
a hireling in the Deity's cosmic yard
the Father tells him what he can and can't
he's allowed these paltry declarations:

"Sorry, this one's going to be quite painful
this one gives you time to say goodbye
this so quick they'll only hear about it
this one you'll see coming by a mile."

I ask about near-deaths who see the Light
he gestures, like it's all phony baloney
but part of his mystique is ambiguity
does he mime that paradise exists?

I think he hopes *I'll* see the light: stop asking
he's never going to tell, though books are written
about the worlds beyond our expiration
"Surmise," he claims, and grins appallingly.

I won't give up, I'll pierce his tawdry veil
trip up God in his bleak censorship
find out precisely who, what, when, where, why
a deathbed journalist, I'll chronicle my own demise.

At Any Moment

We're headed on in to the Kiwanis meeting
and we may not make it to the door
or if we do, we may not last the meeting,
or could fail returning to the car.

So I take your hand in mine
I can feel the very texture of your skin
the roughness where you've worked,
the soft center of your palm.

It is a cheerful blue day, and I make sure
to point it out to you, you smile
and I return it with the most affectionate
glance I can muster given it may be my last

or could be one of many thousands to come
I don't know how to tell you that,
so better keep my apprehension quiet
you swing my arm in yours

with a sense of security that, though false,
I want to allow you on this spring afternoon
because I do not want to remember you
clouded with worry or a sudden sadness.

It could be anytime, I know
from the Kiwanis meeting to our
Sunday afternoon park stroll
and so I want to feel it all.

I want to love you now completely
put aside petty criticisms
open up my heart as much as I can
enjoy you, the good day, the meeting.

I could be leaving you, or you me,
if I hold that in mind, then the sky
will be a richer blue, your smile
will speak of your love fully.

If I told you, you'd think I was morbid
so I say nothing and stop
just outside the Upper Arlington Civic Center
just before we go in to noise and cooling food.

And there I regard you kindly
and kiss you on the lips
and look at you one last time, maybe,
because it could happen at any moment.

A Prayer for the Last Day

When all the dearest people in the world
gather near the last of your frail body
when silent weeping is the order of the night
and footsteps in the courtyard
are the slow and measured pacing of the gravesmen

then your sweet soul will linger
in the room where kneel the dearest of them all
and with silent words and whispers
touches warm but never felt
your old spirit says goodbye
to those she'll meet again
in lives and lives to come.

Then the long and restful journey
the silver cord is broken
up above the moon and mountains
higher than the highest bird
your spirit flies
and in her now

the courage and the constancy
the fiery love she worked to forge
the loyalty, the honesty
the caring heart she gained
continue on and on into the universe
never lost and never mourned.

No death for souls, no darkest night
but arms of all the loving fathers
kingdoms of grace and light
and sleep of peace
until a new awakening.

My Heavens!

I think heaven has streets just like Ames, Iowa
pretty houses all in a row, summer-blue skies.
Is paradise a lot like your hometown?
I think so.

There's a bar on every third corner
otherwise known as a pub, for you English.
They serve cold brews like back on earth
and pretty good morning omelets as well.

All the streets are broad and oak-lined
no need anymore for light industrial areas.
Did I mention there's no National Rifle Association?
No one feels the need to pick up a gun.

There's lots of amenities you'd enjoy, the summer porches,
street festivals on pleasant Sunday afternoons,
there's a carnival down at the park
with Ferris wheels, and thrill rides, and a little gambling.

Did I tell you they don't have hospitals here?
You've learned enough about pain and loss.
Nurses and doctors have another assignment:
they'll coach you on enhancing your bliss.

God is hanging out somewhere up here
he doesn't make a big deal out of his presence
he roams the blossoming alleys in various disguises
making sure every asphalt inch is delightful and semi-orderly.

Do you have your body back? Of course you do!
How else could you smell fresh, planty breezes,
kick that grimy football on an autumn heaven day
or wrap your arms around your ever-willing lover?

Well, lovers, plural, but there's no problem here
you can all amiably share equal time
your ideas about fear and jealousy have vanished
your mind is clear, your heart is steady and wide open.

So what will you do all day? There's joy to share.
And I won't lie, minds are not entirely untroubled
you can give comfort and advice, when asked,
there's still opportunity for your compassion.

You say this is fantasy, and I hear you
but maybe my heaven's just as good as yours
tell me all about your own paradise
there's no competition for Best Celestial Kingdom.

Especially for Poets

You're a Poet — Too Bad for You!

You'll probably never get a book contract
people tell you poetry wastes their time
don't try writing a novel, you've no prose
if you're a poet, it will break your heart.

What if God commissioned you to write only poetry
what if he put those syllables in your brain
in minglements only a poet can assemble,
no fiction or non-fiction order.

Think it a profound and quirky blessing
even if the world turns the other way
even if for months your tongue's becalmed
and every phrase you launch to paper founders.

Heaven never promised you a Hollywood option
nor sway over spirits beyond your own
let ambition fall away into the receptive cosmos
tell yourself: I'm a poet, and that's just fine.

Rejoice in the words that promote your own healing
rest your weary skull in the Poetry Mother's bosom
stop telling yourself it's not your road, your way
here's the truth: you're a poet, that's enough, that's OK.

If you lived in Arabia, they'd worship you
in America, they snicker and sprint away
that doesn't muffle your calling's holiness,
make their indifference fault or sin.

It's a mismatch, you and this cockeyed culture
don't let it spirit your happiness away
sit down, grab your pencil, write the word
that grounds you in your everyday creation.

Poet's Lament

Smack flat dead in words and whispers
all things from my pen rank drivel
shunned by Lady Inspiration
I tug her breast, she won't respond.

Naught but fog within, without
no penny, no poetic thought
body swaying over paper
brain clamped down, de-wired, tripped off.

Is this what they call writer's block?
Then I am writer/indigent/fop
this gleaming autumn won't inspire
my spirit wandered wayward.

They say that cold and dark revive
the scent of cosmic mystery
but here I am, bereft of feeling
hearty face slaps might inspire.

Could trudge to my office warren
punch in phone calls, grin and bear
but I must man these scattered outposts,
noodling nothing, nothing's there.

Someday I hope that Lady fair
will enter, secret, my night chamber
breathe into my ear the mystery
stroke my finger, grant me power.

Then with quill and parchment rough
I'll flash the cosmic spark again
loft my verses heavenward
flame up like a falling star.

Successful Writers All Leave the Midwest

There's a bright cloud over magnificent High Street
and even though successful artists have all left the Midwest
writers to NYC, painters to the Southwest,
the sky ripples and shines here in Columbus, Ohio.

There's an energy that snaps down the boulevards
coming to rest in the calm of Greenlawn cemetery,
circling students who walk to OSU classes,
hanging out in Wendy's, inhabiting morning Cup o' Joe,

tickling the stone-bound molecules
of the Columbus Metropolitan Library
where the ghost of Andrew Carnegie walks,
and he is vitalized by the grand energy

that lights the way for generations of youthful eyes,
soothes anxious parents through empty-house years,
then down into their graves it guides them whole,
made ready for their first faltering step toward infinity.

Those artists, they praise their "Midwest origins"
but they left behind beauty they can now only recall
except that the same light charges down Manhattan streets
roars over the Sangre de Cristo mountains

and wraps us all up, writer and butcher,
into the eternal scheme, no difference among us,
no flyover people, all divisions ceased
in its never-ending peace and power.

To the Writer Turning 70

When they chuck your chin you feel like an ancient
that hang-drop skin, that dissolving barrier,
but I say what the hell, we can live to be 100,
make that our intention, cheat time's erase.

Sure, I know you could "get hit by a truck "
I know we "don't know the hour or the day"
but let's keep a positive attitude, shall we?
Chin up, we've just begun the race.

There's that little matter of embracing yourself completely:
will they lower you into your grave self-flagellating?
Space now for contemplation toward relaxing in the present
don't wrestle impatient with all that happens in time.

Want to end your life vengeful, jeering the enemy dead?
You could use thirty years just to loosen your brainwork chains.
Could you pause for that stink bug crawling on your manuscript
coax him into a catch jar, tap him out soaring?

That's as good as your hypothetical Nobel prize
your concern for that tiny fellow could earn more merit.
You've got life-loving to learn, beyond your cursing
that snob-quarterly rejection, postage price inconvenience.

Your fifty years as networker-novelist have ended
you don't want to gibe with those 40-somethings anyway.
You can make a small effort to stanch the world's suffering
I'll bet there's an opportunity right down your block.

There's a pent-up beagle who needs carefree walking,
an old one like you who could use a grocery lift
so much pain for a laying on of hands
so much sadness wanting a cheerful flower.

Time to journey into your metaphorical deep
you're no more literary/community careerist
jump off the pier into your own private lake
explore its depths until you drown to sorrow.

I'm Serious Serious

I'd write a poem about a weighty subject
but I can't think of a primary object
on which to lavish my wandering attention
to make my bogus statement to the world.

I could write about death, or international torture
but a tortuous composition that would be
because my mind is fixed on silly-lazy-drifting
babbling about spring, me in dead winter's hands.

So I'll be content to whistle down an alleyway
cool and cold under a moon cradled in ice
the local wolf-dog shocking with his howling
I'll walk straight out to the San Diego coast

where houses are a million and the surfy beach is priceless
I can move away from production and travail
there I'll squat beside the cliffs and rolling waves
pick a tune and croon a lay fantastic and delightful.

Till then I'm humble in this chill Midwestern squall
allowing my brain to pool down into my knees
releasing all that pressure like a basketball wheezing
I'm flatulent with breezy words and phrases.

So this is a poem for someone just like me
caught between the stars and a light industrial area
someday verses will trudge by in a chockablock parade
you'll pluck 'em out and pin 'em on your paper.

Packing Up the Bookstore

The day breaks like *Fahrenheit 451*
strewn on the floor, non-fiction and novels
out at the loading zone, poetry molders,
it's all getting prepped for the fire.

What happens to orphan books nobody needs?
They're auctioned and sold for a dollar
trucked to the fairgrounds flea market sale
but what if they linger unwanted?

They're fated to smolder, deep in our wastes
Trollope and Vonnegut, Homer and Collins,
freighted on down to the sulfurous landfill
dumped out with dinner bones into the pit.

And what of the spirits who waltzed in the aisles
of the dear shop they guarded and sanctified?
They'll perish, pushed out on our careless streets:
no room at amazon.com.

The end of a bookshop's a funeral
the U-hauler bears all the corpses along
the bookstore cat howls in her lonely crate,
bookseller vanished long before dawn.

Publish, Perish

I'd like to publish a book of my poetry
a real pretty book nobody will read
I think I'm fairly droll, could inspire
but Billy Collins I'm not, if you please.

A book like old City Lights pocket poets
mini-tome, five bucks, impulse buy
most —you know, fellow poets – are earmarked:
friends sigh forward to oblige.

But now and then a young one approaches
or a senior, cane or walker handy nearby
says: That poem you read, I really like it.
It's in the book? I'd like a copy, sir.

I'm quick to ask: friend, how shall I sign it?
Forget the dollars, it's the obsolete pleasure
of someone feeling I'm a worthy wordsmith,
maybe scan that sonnet one more time.

You know what I'm saying, fellow poets,
we spend our lives declaiming to the breezes
we're not up there reciting on American Idol
we collapse in the gutter, they'll walk on by.

I keep thinking I should live in Arabia
where poets orate rhymes from golden thrones
people journey miles, render homage
memorize the lines to school their kids.

In the Great American Midwest no one cares
poets file in for their very own spotlight
tolerate you mouthing till their open reading
if they buy your book for a buck, kiss their eyes.

But we'll just keep on writing, won't we?
I wouldn't know what else to do
I'd say God has sent me on a mission
but I look behind me, his figure has disappeared.

And I don't "have to write" don't buy
that nonsense spoken by romantics
I could close my computer, open it only
for sports scores, weather bulletins.

But if I didn't write, didn't share, I'd be:
sad and lonely, disabled on my deathbed,
mourning an opportunity abandoned,
someone might have been comforted by my verse.

So I'll power up my pc, you'll open your notebook
we'll scribble along for another few years
maybe heaven's welcoming spirit will enlighten us,
say: Well done. You were sacred in your words.

Best of Fred

Spring Moon

Don't let this moment pass unattended
don't let the spring moon march down the sky alone
an owl is calling from a far oak branch
she is calling you.

Don't let the river journey unaccompanied
put aside your thoughts, let your mind ripple like the river
the sun will be waking, he will require your presence
for his long high arc in tribute to the earth.

Don't let the lark take wing without your witness
she will fall if you, godlike, avert your eyes
she will never sing again if you are unwilling to listen.

Don't let any single moment lose your attention
if you turn away all creation will fail
and when you return you will wonder why you,
like the falling spring moon, are completely alone.

Heaven's Little Western New York Helper

From that "Don't You Worry!" book
to plasticine buddhas molded by coughing Chinese lungs
this country mart in the nowhere town Fredonia, New York
just up the road from my cowgirl sister's manse

strives to be a little lamp that shines
flash-flickering on a narrowing backwoods highway
in deep Chautauqua solitude, all-penetrating Lily Dale light,
Virgin Marys comfortable on its shelves.

This shop foursquare between us and hell's chittering gate
beguiles us with sacred images we'd only profane
while the proprietor ogles a Kirk Douglas champion movie
pounding along on a cable tv wired straight up to high heaven.

This guy says don't ever count out buddhas or polyester virgins
says they haul us awake for the very next round
smack us out of our flagrant dreams
down onto the rough salvation canvas.

Winter Boys

It's the full life of winter's blustery height
ice and flurry and sharp-scented cold
could be mistaken for nature's call to death
but it's character, soft landscape, chill flame.

So we'll pull on big boots and tussle out the door
trek on back to the river frozen deep
jump up and down on the ice until it cracks
walk across water like apprentice Jesus.

Then up along the railroad track, hollering down the valley
teetering on the slippery rails, pounding our chests
at the approaching engine, falling away
at the very last second, down into warm and welcoming drifts.

We pack up solid ice balls, lob them over the precipice
listen for their smack against the distant shivery pavement
then clamber down the hill to the snow-snarled street
dart out suddenly, grab rear bumpers, pogey on the cars.

All the neighbor girls are trying on their delicate skates
they're ready to giggle across the ice in frilly skirts
they need our trusty shoveling to open up reluctant ponds
and that we do, but we disdain their dainty pirouetting.

We're tough guys body-slamming each other on the ice
the pond is a great hibernal wrestling ring
it's only when some peewee warrior cracks his head and wails
that we shrug away from rowdy bickering.

We're headed out for an icy exploit
ready to revel in the frigid winter world
we'll chop and stack an igloo fort, or roll up a snowman,
push in lumps of coal for eyes and a dead carrot nose.

All the frail adults indoors, but this our wild universe
we stride right forward into the knifey wind
breaking a path out back to the trees
and we don't need any big-brother snowshoes.

It's there in the woods that we'll build a fire
with matches purloined from mothers' purses
crisp sticks gathered by our aching mitten hands
suddenly we're warming and invincible.

All around the sky is milky white and falling
not a sound in the little tree grove
our piping voices hushed and still
as the great being of winter embraces our small daring.

To My Brother on His Magic Farm

Honey light healing the bark of trees
shadows drifting toward the sheltering barn
necklaces of flowers, breeze-driven
silence of singing cicadas
sky utterly blue, clouds fairest white

you, my brother, kneeling, working some rough tool,
scraping along the fence, fully concentrated
your old companion, silver hair blessed with sun,
standing swept by wind in her garden
I will know you this way forever.

Here in the comfort of the farm
held by soft and silent hills
you will live beyond my dreams
through all time and ages
I will always come here,
find you standing by.

It could not be
that this sweet place
will one day be no longer
that sky and earth will be erased
and your old bones
lie beneath the tree.

I know the farm dwells forever
its cabbages always bloom,
honeybees find their perfect flower.

I touch you under sunlight radiant like no other
peace enters my body like a river
the hawk circles twice, and flies away.

To My Father, Empowered by a Stroke

Father, I watch you poised beside the bed
trembling against your metal walker
gathering strength for the grand move
to the dressing table across the room.

You will reach that table in minutes
grasp up your electric razor
cock your head back, peer around
the blur of your cataract
earnestly inspect this instrument
that every morning roughs your skin.

You will sit one hour at the table
elaborately shaving your bristly face:
slow movement, finding and pressing the switch
cautious scrubbing atop the beard
opening of the razor's portal,
wire brush, painstaking cleaning
of metal spotless just the day before.

Your life is lived between this bed and table
the twice a day journey down the bathroom hall
it is a good life, filled with meaning and pleasure:

the triumph of your foot arched out and touching
the morning floor, round grip of your hands still
strong against the bedstead, slow haul up
to grip the walker's arms, your smile when you
know that one more time you can make it.

And lying in bed at night, the stories you can tell
all about the old times, when fire balloons filled
the Fourth of July sky, Halley's comet flung itself
across the firmament, you stood watching, spellbound,
in the narrow lanes below.

And when I tell you that grandfather spoke to me
that he will hold your hand and guide you
across the wild expanse of earth and heaven,
you slowly nod your head against the pillow,
close your eyes and whisper
stories of your father and our fathers.

When you sleep I know you dream
of love and light and every radiant glory
then each morning you begin
the ceremony of the razor
firm hand, warm eye, narrow movement
blessing you and me, our slow time together,
our still eternity.

The Book

Did I meet you in that little shop
where the book of love is kept behind the counter?
Impossible, except our names are there
in golden script upon the luminary page.

Who would have thought the string bean boy,
the girl who squats and hops like garden toads
would find each other in the deep immensity
but there you are, my fingers trace your name.

I see mine linked with yours by radiant hearts
the shop's proprietor, his quiet smile,
before the book is closed, takes up the feather pen
turns the page, and writes our names again.

Photo by Mary Rathke/WOSU

Fred Andrle is an Associate at the Ohio State University Humanities Institute. For more than 20 years—until his retirement in May, 2009—he produced and hosted the public affairs talk show "Open Line," heard on WOSU, Columbus. Fred is the recipient of a Thurber House/ Greater Columbus Arts Council Poetry Fellowship (2003) and Playwriting Fellowship (2000). His poetry has been featured on Garrison Keillor's public radio program *The Writer's Almanac* and published in the Columbus Dispatch and in the anthology *Prayers to Protest: Poems that Center and Bless Us* (Pudding House). Fred's poetry collection *Love Life* was published by XOXOX Press in 2008, and in 2011, XOXOX produced the catalog for his joint exhibition with artist Karen Snouffer, called *Love Life—nature and memory at play.*

Fred offers thanks to his fellow House of Toast poets M.J. Abell, Charlene Fix, Jerry Roscoe, Linda Fuller-Smith and Jacquelin Smith for their helpful suggestions and encouragement.